PET CARE FOR KIDS

TURTLES

BY KATHRYN STEVENS

![The Child's World logo]

Published by The Child's World®
1980 Lookout Drive • Mankato, MN 56003-1705
800-599-READ • www.childsworld.com

Acknowledgments
The Child's World®: Mary Berendes, Publishing Director
The Design Lab: Kathleen Petelinsek, Design and Page Production

Photo Credits: Amwu/dreamstime.com: 6; Animalfile/Alamy: 14 (turtle); Arco Images GmbH/Alamy: 8, 9, 11; Areaphotography/dreamstime.com: 7; Bimarto Sasri/dreamstime.com: front cover, back cover (walking); Chode/dreamstime.com: back cover, 18 (hiding); David A. Northcott/Corbis: 15; David Davis/dreamstime: 4, 24; Eric Isselée/dreamstime.com: front cover, 3, 22 (swimming); Irochka/dreamstime.com: 19; iStockphoto.com/Karen Greenstreet: 5; iStockphoto.com/Oktay Ortakcioglu: front cover, back cover, 1, 3, 20 (rock); iStockphoto.com/Tomasz Zachariasz: front cover, back cover, 1, 3, 14, 20 (crickets); iStockphoto.com/TSchon: front cover, 1, 3 (lettuce); iStockphoto.com/Viorika Prikhodko: front cover, 1, 3, 14 (worms); JLP/Jose L. Pelaez/Corbis: 17; Martin Ficalora/dreamstime.com: 13; PhotoDisc: 10; Podius/dreamstime.com: 20 (tank); Thomas Perkins/dreamstime.com: 16; Tony Campbell/dreamstime: front cover, 1, 21 (box)

Library of Congress Cataloging-in-Publication Data
Stevens, Kathryn, 1954–
  Turtles / by Kathryn Stevens.
    p. cm. —(Pet care for kids)
  Includes index.
  ISBN 978-1-60253-187-1 (library bound : alk. paper)
  1. Turtles as pets—Juvenile literature. I. Title. II. Series.
  SF459.T8S74 2009
  639.3'92—dc22   2008040807

Printed in the United States of America
Mankato, Minnesota
September 2009
PA02022

NOTE TO PARENTS AND EDUCATORS

The Pet Care for Kids series is written for children who want to be part of the pet experience but are too young to be in charge of pets themselves. These books are intended to provide a kid-friendly supplement to more detailed information adults need to know about choosing and caring for different types of pets. They can help youngsters learn how to live happily with the animals in their lives, and, with adults' help and supervision, grow into responsible animal caretakers later on.

PET CARE FOR KIDS

CONTENTS

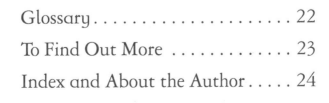

TURTLES AS PETS

Turtles are great animals! But getting a pet turtle is a big decision. Turtles live for many years. They need special care and handling. Some states even have laws about keeping them. People who want pet turtles should learn all about them first.

▶ This baby painted turtle is too small to buy as a pet. It is against the law to sell turtles smaller than 4 inches (10 centimeters). And turtles should never be taken from the wild.

◀ Many turtles can live for 40 years or more. Eastern box turtles like this one sometimes live to be 100!

WATER OR LAND?

Many turtles live mostly in water. Water turtles swim very well. Other turtles live mostly on land. Box turtles and **tortoises** are land turtles. Land turtles cannot swim well. In deeper water, they can drown!

▶ This red-eared slider swims very well. Its feet act like swim fins.

◀ Radiated tortoises like this one live on land. Their bodies are not made for swimming.

A NICE HOME

Different turtles need different kinds of homes. All turtles need dry places for resting. And they need a food dish. Water turtles need water for swimming. They often live in clear tanks called **aquariums**. A **filter** helps keep the water clean.

▶ This Florida redbelly turtle has a place to swim. It also has places to climb out of the water.

▼ It can be hard to make good homes for water turtles. They might not be good pets for beginners.

Pet land turtles often live in big wood or plastic boxes. These turtles do not need deep water for swimming. They need shallow water to sit in and drink. They also need somewhere to hide. They like to have a place to dig. Potting soil or special **bedding** are good for digging.

This pet box turtle has a nice outdoor home. Box turtles can be hard to keep indoors.

Many land turtles like digging in soft potting soil like this.

WARMTH

Turtles need outside heat to warm their bodies. Part of the turtle's home should be warmer. A light or heat lamp can keep it warm. A water heater can warm the swimming water. Other parts of the turtle's home stay cooler. The turtle can choose the right spot.

▸ Outside, turtles lie in the sun to warm up. They cool off in the shade or in the water.

GOOD FOOD

Different turtles need different foods.

Pet stores sell special turtle foods.

Tortoises eat fruits and vegetables.

Water turtles and box turtles also love

worms and insects. People with pet

turtles need to learn what foods to

use. Adding special powders can make

foods even better.

▶ This Eastern box turtle is eating an earthworm. Turtles must be warm enough to eat. If they are cold, they cannot break down food.

◀ This Greek turtle is eating lettuce.

SAFETY

Many turtles carry germs. These germs can make people very ill. Handwashing is important. So is cleaning the turtle's home. Good food helps turtles stay healthy, too. But sometimes turtles need to see animal doctors, or **vets**.

▸ This teacher is helping students handle a turtle safely.

◂ People should always wash up after handling a turtle. And very young children should not handle turtles at all.

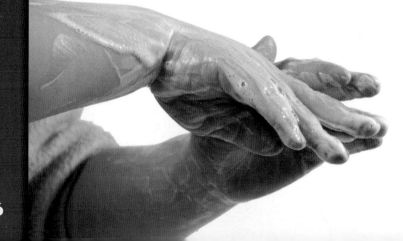

LOVING CARE

Turtles do not like to cuddle. They do not like to be petted. And they need special care. But they are very interesting. For some people, turtles can be great pets. And they can be great pets for many, many years!

This red-eared slider's owner has taken very good care of her.

This turtle got scared. He is hiding inside his shell.

NEEDS:

* the right kind of home
* a clean home
* clean water
* places to rest or hide
* a food dish
* the right foods
* sunlight or special lights

DANGERS:

* getting too hot, cold, or dry
* a dirty home
* no water
* the wrong foods
* poisonous plants
* getting dropped
* getting loose
* other animals
* soap or cleaners

SHELL:
A broken shell hurts!
And it can make
the turtle sick.

EYES:
Turtles can see
very well.

MOUTH:
Turtles do not have
teeth. They use their
sharp beaks to bite
and chew.

SHELL:
Turtles have a hard
shell. They cannot
take it off.

CLAWS:
Turtles have small,
sharp claws.

KINDS:
There are over 250
kinds of turtles.

GLOSSARY

aquariums (*uh-KWAYR-ee-ums*) Aquariums are clear tanks where animals can live.

bedding (*BED-ding*) Bedding for turtles is something they can dig in.

filter (*FIL-tur*) An aquarium filter cleans dirt and food out of the water.

tortoises (*TOR-tuh-suz*) Tortoises are turtles that live mostly on land.

vets (*VETS*) Vets are doctors who take care of animals. Vet is short for "veterinarian" (*vet-rih-NAYR-ee-un*).

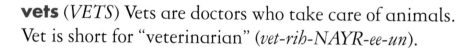

TO FIND OUT MORE

Books:

Haney, Johannah. *Turtles*. New York: Marshall Cavendish Benchmark, 2008.

Randolph, Joanne. *Turtles*. New York: PowerKids Press, 2007.

Schafer, Susan. *Turtles*. New York: Marshall Cavendish Benchmark, 1999.

Wilke, Hartmut. *My Turtle and Me*. New York: Barron's Educational Series, 2005.

Video/DVD:

Paws, Claws, Feathers & Fins: A Kid's Guide to Happy, Healthy Pets. Goldhil Learning Series (Video 1993, DVD 2005).

Web Sites:

Visit our Web page for lots of links about pet care:
http://www.childsworld.com/links

Note to parents, teachers, and librarians: We routinely verify our Web links to make sure they are safe, active sites—so encourage your readers to check them out!

INDEX

ABOUT THE AUTHOR
Kathryn Stevens has authored and edited many books for young readers, including books on animals ranging from grizzly bears to fleas. She's a lifelong pet-lover and currently cares for a big, huggable pet-therapy dog named Fudge.